Behind The Door

A Chaplain's Story

Dee Pulliam

BEHIND THE DOOR: A CHAPLAIN'S STORY

DP Ministries

deepulliamministries@gmail.com

Publication Services:

Rev/12 Publishing

211 Harriet Tubman Street

Knoxville, TN 37915

www.overcomingbelieverschurch.org

office@overcomingbelieverschurch.org

Editor: Ogletre Editing

attms2@gmail.com

Cover Design and Publication:

NITT Tech Services

nitttechservices@gmail.com

Cover and Chapter Images:

Photo 92415454 © Kevin Carden | Dreamstime.com;

Photo 35127865 © Ig0rzh | Dreamstime.com;

PrettyPresetsByJess:

https://www.etsy.com/people/0d8u4zely2jyymsz?ref=shop_home_header

Printed in the United States of America

ISBN: 979-8-218-49005-8

Independently Published

DEDICATION

I dedicate this work to my girls, Raven Breanna and Tiara Christine, who are the delight of my heart.

CONTENTS

	Acknowledgments	viii
	Forward	x
	Introduction	1
Chapter 1	A Door of Beginning	5
Chapter 2	A Door of What's Next	15
Chapter 3	A Door of Adulting is Hard	25
Chapter 4	A Door of Promise	35
Chapter 5	A Door of Loss	45
Chapter 6	A Door of Tests	55
Chapter 7	A Door of Change	65
Chapter 8	A Door of Solitude	75
Chapter 9	A Door of Chaplaincy	89
Chapter 10	A Door of "Do It Again" Lord	101
	Conclusion	111
	About the Author	113
	Other Rev/12 Publications	115

ACKNOWLEDGMENTS

To my Raven: You are the joy of my heart. Thank you for loving me and our girls so unselfishly. I am grateful to do life with you. What an exceptional dad you are, too. Thank you, precious.

To my Raven Breanna and Tiara Christine: You are the fulfillment of my heart's desires. I prayed and asked the Lord for you. You make me happy. I am so proud of you and the beautiful women you have become. I am forever grateful to be able to say that I am your mom.

To Pastor Jerry W. Doss: You are the first to ever speak over me about a pastoral anointing on my life. I remember the uncertainty in my mind, yet also the inner witness in my heart. How amazing to have served for nineteen years at Abundant Faith Christian Center, Springfield, IL! For the many years of sacrifice and serving together at AFCC, I want to say a "special" thank you.

To Pastor Daryl W. Arnold: We may have just met, but it is as if I have known you for a very long time. Yes, indeed, bloodline. In this season, we are grateful to have the opportunity to serve under your leadership at Overcoming Believers Church, Knoxville, TN. Every week, we come away from service inspired and transformed by the word of God, "I got that, Pastor!"

To every patient: That I have had the privilege of entering Behind the Door and into your room. I am forever grateful for the lessons learned and that you would open the door of your heart to share your life's story, your tears, and on many occasions the fear of the hard place that you faced.

FORWARD

If you are looking for an easy read that helps you navigate through the multiplicity of life's seasons and need encouragement when you are treading through life's inevitable unexpected turns and twists, then this is the book for you. Dee Pulliam has an uncanny way of marrying theological truths with practical stories in order to bring clarity to God's direction in our lives. Her many testimonies of God's faithfulness will be helpful nuggets of wisdom that will undoubtedly encourage you in your own faith journey.

Pastor Daryl W. Arnold

Senior Pastor

Overcoming Believers Church

Knoxville, TN

INTRODUCTION

I dreamed of writing a book many years ago, yet it had been removed from my mind. This is how this book came to fruition.

It was early Saturday morning, and my spouse had gone fishing for striped bass. I was sitting on our screened-in deck with the birds chirping. There was a slight breeze, and the sun was shining. I honestly felt like I could have slept a little longer, but more than that, I have come to yearn for these quiet moments with God. Typically for me, I have a cup of caramel vanilla coffee, my daily devotional, and my journal.

As I sat there, my mind began to reflect on the many different patient encounters I had experienced over the years as a hospital Chaplain. I was flooded with thoughts of what was ***"Behind the Door"*** in those situations. I envisioned a hallway with several doors. I could then see an Emergency Department filled with the hustle and bustle of medical personnel as another trauma patient was brought in. There has been a shooting, and a lockdown is in place with police presence everywhere. My heart prepares for when I will meet the family of the victim. I began to write.

As I continued to sit in the Lord's presence, I could hardly write fast enough because thoughts kept flooding my mind. I knew He was with me, and I did not want to miss this special moment.

First things first, Christ said I am the door. ***"Then Jesus said to them again, Most assuredly I say to you, I am the door of the sheep."*** **John 10:7 NKJV**

Like a sheep, I, too, wandered from place to place, lost and desperate to find my way, needing a Shepherd to guide me. Finding Christ has led me to the door of purpose for my life.

The reflections in the pages that follow will be my personal life story. We will look at life from the perspective of a series of doors. Some I admit I willingly walked through, and others…well… circumstances drove me through them.

Together, let us discover what is ***"Behind the Door."***

For I know the plans I have for you, declares the Lord, plans to prosper you and not to harm you, plans to give you hope and a future.

Jeremiah 29:11 NIV

CHAPTER 1: A DOOR OF BEGINNING

We do not get to choose our family or the circumstances around which we are born. Yet, we do all have a beginning. Here is the start of mine.

I was raised in a two-parent home, and we lived on the east side in the projects. You know, the red brick row homes. If we were poor, I really did not know it because there was always something to eat. It may not have been what you wanted, but we learned to eat what was placed in front of you. When we did not like it and refused to eat, for example, the salmon croquettes I hated, we were just sent to bed hungry. My mom did not play about that. There were talks about commodity cheese, powdered milk, and my older siblings even having to share the same bath water, but as a child, I did not think about those things.

Mom always kept our home neat and clean. The linoleum floors were freshly mopped and shiny from being waxed. I remember it like it was yesterday.

Outside were beautiful flowers that mom loved; marigolds and peonies, to name a couple. On the inside though, there was often chaos and dysfunction in the house, mainly because my parents argued, which resulted in lots of yelling, cussing, and sometimes even physical fights.

There were seven kids, and I was the youngest baby girl. Plus, I had five stepbrothers and sisters from dad's previous marriage. Several years separated me from my older siblings, who were often busy, leaving me feeling like I did not have a sense of much guidance. I learned early how to stay out of the way, obey the rules, and hopefully not incur mom's wrath. The goal was to avoid getting a whooping. The kind of whooping that if they happened today, Child Protective Services would remove you from the home. It always started with, "Go get me a switch," and you knew you were in trouble.

At best, I fumbled through school, not feeling like I was as smart as others. It seemed I either could not understand or could not retain what I had learned.

Then, a serious bike accident in grade school left me with a chipped tooth. I was self-conscious and did not feel as pretty as my sisters or other girls. Plus, I hated my unmanageable, kinky hair that my mom liked to style with a part down the middle and put into two cornrows. Ironically, things have come full circle, and today that style is very popular with weave hair braided in.

My grandparents gave me my Baptist heritage. My earliest memories of the Lord are of when I heard Jesus was coming back. I vividly recall sitting on the steps of our apartment in the projects and looking up at the sky. While I did not know Him, I knew Jesus represented someone good, and when He came, I planned to wave at Him to get His attention.

Was He the answer to get me out of all the chaos? Was He the answer to help me like myself?

At home, every time I would be called out of my name, defiance would rise up on the inside of me, and I would say to myself, "B**ch, is not my name." I do not know where that fight on the inside came from. As a little girl, I promised myself that when I had my own kids, I would never call them out of their names.

Many years would pass before I fully understood that the Lord already saw me. Hagar declared that when she cried out to Him in her distress, the Lord spoke to her, and in response, she said, ***"You are the God who sees me."*** **Genesis 16:13 NIV.**

I got married at the age of eighteen. I had just turned eighteen only three days before. I know now it was an attempt to escape from home. He was a PK (preacher's kid). But even the sacredness of that could not help us to survive the pitfalls. The marriage was doomed from the start. We married way too early, and we were way too young. Our love alone was not enough to navigate through the uncertainties of life. We married, divorced, re-married, and divorced again in a span of five years.

It was all so cruel and left me empty and broken. Life can hit you that hard sometimes. I know it was meant to destroy me completely, and it almost did. If you have never been there, well, just keep on living and let life happen.

This brokenness and the fact that my ex-spouse died in an auto accident a short time after our final divorce was more than I could bear. At the funeral, I was not even allowed to sit with the family. I was not his wife. I was nobody. He died before I could say how sorry I truly was and before I could ask for his forgiveness for my part in what went wrong. This loss drove me into a downward spiral with thoughts of suicide. In desperation, I turned to the only One who could turn my life around.

One day, He did just that as I sat on the couch in my one-bedroom apartment and cried, "God help me!" I had been attending a Baptist church, but my lifestyle was far from right. Weekend binges of drugs, alcohol, and partying were all I lived for.

I sat down and turned to **Romans 10:9-10 NIV:**

"If you declare with your mouth, Jesus is Lord, and believe in your heart that God raised Him from the dead, you will be saved. For it is with your heart that you believe and are justified, and it is with your mouth that you profess your faith and are saved."

My prayer was simple: "Lord, help me. I have made such a mess of things. I do believe. I give you my heart. Please forgive me. I surrender. I confess you as Lord. I receive you now, in Jesus' name."

I can mark that moment at 107 West Lawrence when my life was radically changed, at least for a while. Not totally at first, because the drugs were a real battle. When I slipped up, though, the conviction was immediate.

Wherever you may find yourself, the Door of Beginnings has great significance. Zechariah 4:10 (paraphrase) tells us not to despise the day of small beginnings. However small it is, at least it is a start. Hold on to that and know that this door is the one that leads to all the others. There will be opposition and opportunities to give up, but He sees you and is with you.

Many, many years later, I witnessed the dysfunction of my childhood home being turned around to one of surrender as both of my parents found salvation in Christ. In their senior years, they were more settled and became my best friends. I loved them dearly.

One Sunday, my dad walked down the aisle at church in answer to the altar call and gave his heart to Jesus. I had not even realized he was there in attendance.

Then, my mom prayed with me to receive Jesus as her personal Lord and Savior while we were driving down the highway on a sunny day. I asked her, "Mom, have you ever thought about going to heaven?" She responded, "Well, yes, baby, but you never know." I shared the truth of the Gospel with her. After we prayed the prayer of salvation together, it sure seemed to me that the sun was brighter, and the sky was even more blue. What a glorious day. Only God!

Chapter 1 – Behind The Door - Beginning

You are more than what you have been through in life. How amazing it is to think that the God of the universe has plans for you and me. Even when we were the furthest from him, He yet had thoughts of hope and a future for us.

What is your earliest memory of God?

Write a letter of reflection to God – Behind the Door - Beginning

Commit to the Lord whatever you do, and he will establish your plans.

Proverbs 16:3 NIV

CHAPTER 2: A DOOR OF WHAT'S NEXT

I was traumatized. A failed marriage, promiscuity, drugs, depression, confusion, and thoughts of suicide. I was the wretched person in:

***"Oh, what a miserable person I am! Who will free me from this life that is dominated by sin and death?"* Romans 7:24 NLT**

Another relationship was not the answer. There had been many. Another high was not the answer because it did not last. The escalation of drug use became alarming. I took a hit of acid one day before going to work. What a ridiculous and reckless thing to do. Yet, what scared me was that I liked how it made me feel. It was in this broken place that I began to cry out to God for real, for real this time.

***"Whoever conceals their sins does not prosper, but the one who confesses and renounces them finds mercy."* Proverbs 28:13 NIV**

It had been His mercy all along that kept me. I had begun to ask God where was the power to live in victory like the Bible says. I was singing in the choir on Sunday and smoking dope on Monday. Even in my sin and half-heartedness, I knew there had to be more to life.

God, will you? God, can you deliver me?

One night, while kneeling on the hardwood floors of that Baptist church, my Bible fell open to:

***"For I know the plans I have for you," declares the Lord, "plans to prosper you and not to harm you, plans to give you hope and a future."* Jeremiah 29:11 NIV**

Oh, my goodness, had I ever even read that before? God had plans for me and thought well of me. Me? Okay, so no more playing church then. I could not continue the back and forth. Despite how I had made a mess of things and after all I had done, and despite my own shame being more than I could bear because I had not kept my promises to Him. God had good things for me. It was so hard to believe, yet it was as if the words lifted off the page and literally pierced my heart.

Jeremiah does not end there…

Vs. 12 Then you will call on me and come and pray to me, and I will listen to you.

Vs. 13 You will seek me and find me when you seek me with all your heart.

I embraced these words as the answer to my cry because I had not been earnestly seeking Him. Not really. I had not come to an end of the misery until now.

I gave God permission to shut whatever door He chose, and I committed to seek Him with all my heart. Quickly, things began to come into alignment. What I had no strength or sense to walk away from, God shut the door. Thank you, Lord!

He took away the desire for the drugs. People who were a bad influence on me moved out of town. I learned to distance myself from people and places that triggered my repeated falling, and my life began to move forward with momentum in a whole new way.

***"I will not merely walk, but run the way of your commandments, when you give me a heart that is willing."* Psalm 119:32 AMPC**

During this time in my life, the Lord sent me a mentor who opened her heart and home to me. At church, she would sit in the balcony with her hands raised, and she praised the Lord with such exuberance. She was always so loud, and I am sure she annoyed some people at church. Yet, her life was evidence of something I did not have. Through her example and our Bible study together, I would come to understand and receive the baptism of the Holy Spirit.

***"If you then, though you are evil, know how to give good gifts to your children, how much more will your Father in heaven give the Holy Spirit to those who ask him!"* Luke 11:13 NIV**

The only qualifier was to simply ask. I did not have to be someone important. I did not have to have a certain title or position in the church. This good gift was for me, and my heart rejoiced in that. I had a beautiful encounter with God one night after leaving my friend's home. I had one hand on the steering wheel and the other hand raised to the Lord. I prayed, "I want all that you have for me." As I began to thank Him, a language I had never heard came out of my mouth. I prayed in this language all the way home. I entered my apartment and went into the bathroom to look in the mirror and try to see the words coming out of my mouth. It was me, but the words were not me, and I knew it was God. This infilling catapulted my walk with the Lord and my prayer life. I have never been the same since.

I fondly remember my dear friend Beverly. We used to sit around the piano, sing, and worship the Lord together. Not to mention the delicious fried chicken, cabbage, sweet potatoes, and cornbread. Oh, my goodness!

Beverly has since gone on to be with the Lord, but her witness and life spoke volumes to me. She taught me the importance of how to wait on the Lord.

These also were the early days of my longing to play the piano (more on that later) because she played so beautifully.

Here is an inscription that she wrote in a topical concordance of the Bible that she gave me:

"Seek Him as a desperate person needing to find the only answer. What you need is in His Word alone. Do not just wait for the answer – dig deep – you are sure to find it. You will not be disappointed. Endless hours spent searching will be worth the treasure you will find. He is priceless, I tell you, and that is the truth. Nothing else can begin to equal – no success, joy, or happiness unless found in Him!"

These words have proven to be true over the years. Thank you, Beverly, my dear friend, for teaching me the lessons of waiting in His presence, for showing me how to pray, and for teaching me the power of praise and worship.

My life has forever changed. Here are words from a hymn that we use to sing, "A Charge to Keep I Have" by Charles Wesley, pub. 1762:

A charge to keep I have,
A God to glorify,
A never-dying soul to save,
And fit it for the sky.

To serve the present age,

My calling to fulfill,

Oh, may it all my powers engage

To do my Master's will!

Stepping through the Door of What's Next comes with relinquishing our need to be in control. We must understand that He alone is God. We cannot bypass the process, but we can be assured that He is well-able to get us to the other side.

Chapter 2 – Behind the Door – What's Next

To totally surrender is not an easy thing. It requires trusting that God really knows what He is doing. The best place to be in is in His perfect will.

Can you mark the spot in your life when you surrendered to God for real?

Write a letter of reflection to God – Behind the Door - What's Next

May all who seek you rejoice and be glad in you; may those who long for your saving help say, "The Lord is Great!" But as for me, I am poor and needy; come quickly to me, oh God. You are my help and my deliverer. Lord do not delay.

Psalm 70:4-5 NIV

CHAPTER 3: A DOOR OF ADULTING IS HARD

I credit my daughters for this chapter title. It is an expression they would use when transitioning from high school to college.

It is true that I had gotten saved, but I was still young. At times, it was extremely hard to honor my commitment to the Lord. Has anybody else ever been there? I had to be disciplined to not go down a particular street or to a particular house so I would not fall back into the same pitfalls. I had to learn not to be around certain people who made it easy for me to make the wrong choices. I had to learn to avoid triggers that would set me back even after months of being drug-free. The cycle of sin and guilt, I believe, was indeed broken, yet the challenge now was to walk in that freedom.

My church membership changed from the Baptist church to a non-denominational, faith-based church. This was the start of even more victorious living. I enrolled in Bible School, which entailed attending classes three to four nights per week. Renewing my mind with the word of God and having accountability with others made the difference.

Around this time, I even had the joy of joining a praise team and leading worship for the first time at church. Worship would continually be an integral part of my life. When I stood before the people to lead them in worship, it just fit me, and the anointing quickly became evident. Amazing doors of favor had opened for me.

In the years to come, worship would remain an anchor for me to stay free as I served in the local church.

I vowed during this time that I would not have sex again with anyone unless he were my husband. I had gone to a Kenneth Copeland Ministries conference in TX, and the teaching was from **Romans 12:1-2 NIV:**

"Therefore, I urge you, brothers and sisters, in view of God's mercy, to offer your bodies as a living sacrifice, holy and pleasing to God – this is your true and proper worship. Do not conform to the pattern of this world, but be transformed by the renewing of your mind. Then you will be able to test and approve what God's will is – His good, pleasing and perfect will."

I marvel at how my whispered promises to God would come to pass. I did not want to disappoint Him or myself ever again. As far as I knew, it would be just me and Jesus forever.

Deeper Bible study, evangelism classes, witnessing door-to-door, and fellowship with other believers had me fired up to tell everyone about the goodness of God and the love and forgiveness I had found. Something very significant happened during this time.

It was December 1984 and an unseasonably warm day. After church, I went to the park with a girlfriend for a walk. While walking, we came across two guys jogging toward us. It was not anybody we knew, but I simply smiled, and we kept walking. That seemingly chance encounter would lead to seeing one of those guys in the grocery store a week later. He approached me and mentioned he had seen me in the park. I was initially irritated because he was flirting, and it was supposed to be just me and Jesus. I was not interested. As he tells it, he remembered my smile from when we passed each other in the park the week before.

The irony is that he was in the food service industry at the time, and the parmesan cheese at his restaurant had molded. He said that never happens. This was no chance encounter. Here we are now at the same store, at the same time and in the same checkout line. Before leaving, I handed him a gospel track and my business card. This well-timed door would change my life completely.

He went back to the restaurant and showed the guys my business card (not the gospel track). Later that same evening, he called me. A male friend of mine answered the telephone. He said that was a surprise, to say the least.

Yet back then, as a way for us to stay set apart and keep each other accountable, the young adult group would often have Bible study and hang out together. That evening, I had several friends from our church young adult group over to my apartment.

I was handed the phone, and during the conversation, I invited him to church. The next day was Sunday. He later told me that if I had invited him to a traditional church, he would have had no interest in attending. Yet, this faith-based church intrigued him, and he accepted the invitation.

That Sunday, we had a guest speaker. What a divine set-up. At the end of the service, and to the delight of everyone, he responded to the altar call and gave his heart to Christ.

When he left after church, I remember thinking it would be nice if he were someone for me. Yet, I had no trust that he was and left it at that. He would come back that same day for the night service.

This special someone began attending the church, and the people began to pray for us to be a couple. Maybe, too, because there were only a few African Americans in a predominately white church. Grandma Carver would tell me he was the one. I was resistant at first. Only God knew His plans.

We would hang out together in our youth group. Eventually, we started dating. I gave him a Bible teaching tape series on Faith, and he prayed and asked the Lord if I could be his wife.

Today, that special someone is my spouse of thirty-eight years. A bonus for me was that he would later go off to culinary school to become a certified Executive Chef. Talk about God is in the details. I was out of Bible School by then. When we met, for me, it was either church, Bible study, and/or I played in two softball leagues a week with tournaments on the weekend. All I had in the refrigerator was a pitcher of water. Surely, there was something else in the fridge, but I honestly cannot think of what that was.

Putting the Kingdom first pays off, and witnessing to him blessed me with someone who loved the Lord, was committed, a Chef, and someone who would become an amazing father to our girls.

Adulting does not happen automatically. The true transition of adulting can be and is hard. You will make mistakes. You will have to have perseverance and keep pressing. Each time you fall, though, get back up.

Jeremiah 32:17 NIV tells us ***"Ah, Sovereign Lord, you have made the heavens and the earth by your great power and outstretched arm. Nothing is too hard for you."***

Let me submit it to you like this. For every hard place in your life, look to Him. He is there. This amazing God who got me through so many difficult seasons will also see you through.

He will allow your dreams to come to pass out of the ashes of nothing. This Door allowed us to see God's hand on us. We could see how well He orchestrated everything and set us up to meet.

The hardship was in surrendering, waiting, and letting His plan unfold. Finally, it had all turned around.

Chapter 3 – Behind the Door – Adulting is Hard

The Lord has proven time and time again that He was with me. He is with you too. I love that we serve a God who delights in surprising us.

Is there a surprise or season in your life where things turned out differently than you planned?

Write a letter of reflection to God – Behind the Door – Adulting is Hard

He remembers his covenant forever, the promises

He made for a thousand generations.

Psalm 105:8 NIV

CHAPTER 4: A DOOR OF PROMISE

Standing on the promises of God is a faith walk indeed. It seemed like we had to fight for every promise. Have you ever been there? In fact, you may be in a fight right now.

A year after we met, we were married in the same church I invited him to. It seems like others saw we would be together before we did and kept telling us, "Told you so." We were so happy and excited.

***"What, then, shall we say in response to these things? If God is for us, who can be against us."* Romans 8:31 NIV**

A big challenge for us now was managing our money. Financial hardships were prevalent at first. We both worked, but we were often overextended in our finances. We now know that financial stewardship, living within your means, sowing, and saving are so important.

One particularly tough time that stands out is when we were between paychecks. We had this piggy bank—literally, a pink pig with a plug in the bottom of it. We broke it open over the bed and spilled out the contents. What was inside came to about twenty dollars.

We were so excited. Twenty dollars was a lot back then because you had a few dollars for church, gas, McDonald's and still had some change left over. Say amen if you know what I am talking about.

Today, we are so grateful that God led us to career choices where work could always be found. Raven's profession is that of a chef. I have an extensive background in administrative support and can multitask with ease. Things eventually got better as we strived to put God first in our finances.

Little did I know back then that the state job I started as a clerk-typist thirty-two years later would result in a monthly retirement check. God always makes a way. I believe He will for you, too. Seek counsel about where you are financially. The discipline to spend some and save some took us years. Live within your means. Ask the Lord, and He will show you how. A promise to stand on is ***"But my God shall supply all your need according to His riches in glory in Christ Jesus."*** **Phil. 4:19 KJV**

Then, after a few years of marriage, more than anything, my heart longed to be a mom. I would confess it and pray about it every day. We were busy and serving in church, but this was always in the back of my mind. I was active in worship and prison outreach ministry. A team of us would travel statewide to various correctional facilities for men and women to bring worship, skits, and preach the gospel to the inmates. As far back as I can remember, my heart has longed to go to places where people were hurting.

***"Take delight in the Lord and he will give you the desires of your heart."* Psalm 37:4 NIV**

This is one of the Bible verses I stood on. It took nine years for this Door of Promise of becoming a mom to open. At times, I would waiver in my belief, and some days, it was immeasurably difficult. We went to the doctor, and I grew to hate the word infertile. But, oh, the promises of God. When you have done all that you know to do to stand, simply stand. We eventually conceived our first baby girl.

We quickly learned, though, that once you receive your promise, do not put your armor away because you will still need it.

At nineteen weeks pregnant, on an Easter weekend, I began to have contractions and went into labor. It resulted in my being hospitalized. How could this be? This was our promise. God, surely you will not let her be taken from us?

My mind was in a whirlwind. I battled unbelief as images of a little casket would bombard my mind. I would resist those thoughts by speaking the word.

While hospitalized, I will never forget that a young intern doctor entered the room. We had already changed rooms more than once, inching me closer and closer to the actual delivery room. He introduced himself and said, "I will be with you when you have your baby tonight." In my drug-induced state, I replied, "It is nice to meet you, but you will not be with me tonight because this is my promise. It is too early, and she will not come tonight!"

Only God! What is that impossible thing in your life that you need from the Lord right now? I am a witness that He can, and He will do it. Let me submit to you that He specializes in the impossible.

Eventually, the contractions were brought under control. I was placed on bed rest and released to go home from the hospital. We took a step of faith and set up the nursery at home. We ordered a gliding rocking chair that I still have to this day. I am sitting in it now as I write.

I would sit in that chair and envision myself rocking her. Sometimes, I would dance in our baby girl's room with a teddy bear in my arms and make myself believe despite the threat of more contractions.

"For nothing will be impossible with God." **Luke 1:37 ESV**

No matter the circumstances, look to the Lord. No matter how hard it seems, lay that impossibility at His feet.

If our baby girl had been born when I began to have those contractions at nineteen weeks, she would not be here today. By faith, I made myself envision holding her, seeing her go to school, and seeing her grow up. She was our promise.

Financially, in this situation, God provided, too, because I had enough accumulated paid time off at work to be off with pay until she was born. Bedrest at nineteen weeks, and she did not deliver until thirty-nine weeks. By the time she was born, I was asking the doctor to get her out because I was tired, swollen, and miserable.

Today, our beautiful baby girl is twenty-nine. She is a Fashion Design major, adventurous, talented, and has a heart of compassion for others. She is at the age now that she speaks truth back into my life. How amazing it is to have almost lost her, and now she speaks the word of God back to me. Thank you, Lord. I am forever grateful.

There is so much to learn when becoming a first-time mom. I cried when breastfeeding because at first my nipples were so sore. The pain was unbearable, and I did not think I would ever survive that, but I did.

I had no clue what to do with her hair and had to have another mom teach me how to braid it. I had to grow in grace and patience through all the sleepless nights, struggles, and surprises along the way.

Then, I remember telling my husband there was one more. If you were to ask me, how did you know? Well, it was just something I knew on the inside. Three years later, when I handed him the pregnancy test, he asked how did that happen? Need I say more? I told him so. Another beautiful promise. When she was born, I immediately knew our family was complete.

Our youngest daughter is just as amazing and is a Chemistry major. She is now twenty-six, smart, and analytical. My daughters are complete opposites in so many ways. Yet, that is what delights my heart and makes everything even more interesting.

One calls me Mom, and the other Ma. To this day, my heart still leaps with joy when I hear them call me that.

I do not take it for granted, and I cherish them. I am reminded that this is a Door only God could open. His blessing of provision and His blessing of my girls.

"For all the promises of God in Him are yes, and in Him amen, to the glory of God through us." **II Cor. 1:20 NKJV**

Chapter 4 - Behind the Door - Promises

I am forever grateful for the Lord's faithfulness in meeting our needs and giving us a healthy family.

What delights your heart in God? What promises has He already fulfilled?

Write a letter of reflection to God – Behind the Door - Promises.

The Lord is close to the brokenhearted and saves those who are crushed in spirit.

Psalm 34:18 NIV

CHAPTER 5: A DOOR OF LOSS

It was May 2008, and nothing could have prepared me for this door.

I was very active in ministry and leading the Music and Fine Arts Department at church. Busy, almost to a fault and consumed with church work. In reflecting back, I had no sense of balance whatsoever. All that mattered was my calling, or so I thought.

My dad became ill, and my sister recognized that he needed to go to the hospital. When I arrived, my mom and sister had taken him to ER. I expected that he would be assessed, get some meds, and then be released to go home.

It is important to note that during this time, other serious family dynamics were taking place. I choose not to elaborate on them simply out of respect and love for those involved. To say that it all was overwhelming is putting it mildly. Nothing could prepare any of us for what was about to come.

Dad ended up needing to be hospitalized because test results revealed he had more than one mini-stroke. Eventually, the entire family was called in to meet with the Palliative Care team to determine what was next.

Then, we found out on an early Saturday morning call from the hospital that dad had had another stroke in the night. This was a big one. Also, he was combatting the early stages of dementia. Within a week, our family was faced with a decision to put dad on hospice care, and he was placed on a special hospice care unit. I could not fully comprehend what all this meant. It felt like a dream. Can somebody please wake me?

Emotionally and physically, I was exhausted. That week my daily routine was to get my girls ready for their day and off to school. I do not know what I would have done without my spouse to lean on. After dropping off the girls at school, I would work in the morning and head to the hospital in the afternoon. I still think that during this time, I was in denial. Tests of this magnitude will cause that.

In the evening, the nurse would come in, lotion his back, and speak kindly to him. Dad could not speak now from the stroke, but his crooked smile let us know he liked the back rubs. He also knew I was there. The nurse would then give him his nightly dose of morphine. As he would fall asleep, I would tell him repeatedly how much I loved him. I would kiss him on the cheek and say, "I'll see you tomorrow, daddy." But my heart feared because there was so much uncertainty about how many more tomorrows we would have. I whispered to the Lord, "God, please."

I was comforted by the fact that before the stroke, I had a conversation with my dad and reminded him of God's love for him and the assurance of salvation in Christ. Before the stroke, my spouse and I were even making plans to take him home to our house to care for him. Yet, that would not be how things would turn out. One response I remember hearing on the inside from the Lord was, "Hold On."

Those two words were on repeat inside of me. Those two words carried me through dad's passing and the ensuing weeks of trying to move forward without him.

One evening, while at my dad's bedside, I recall a Chaplain entering the room. She wore a blue jacket. She handed me a navy-blue blanket with the hospital's logo on it. She said, "We're visiting all the families in hospice tonight, and we wanted you to know we care." I cannot even remember her name, her face, or even if she prayed. All I remember is that the blanket symbolized to me that God saw me. All I remember is that her words brought ease to my heart.

In my exhaustion, the tangible comfort I received in those moments meant everything. I wrapped the blanket around me and decided to stay a little while longer with dad that evening.

Without a doubt, I believe the seeds of chaplaincy were planted in me that night.

"Praise be to the God and Father of our Lord Jesus Christ, the Father of compassion and the God of all comfort, who comforts us in all our troubles, so that we can comfort those in any trouble with the comfort we ourselves receive from God." **II Corinthians 1:3-5 NIV**

Dad passed away within a week, and I had never felt such pain before. My stomach would be in knots leading up to the day of the funeral. I was physically ill. The day of the funeral, I told the Lord I did not want to go but knew I had to. This door is one I would have closed if I had the choice. It is one that only by the grace of God's "Hold On" was I able to make it.

If you have ever faced loss yourself, you understand. Please be comforted by the fact that in your greatest moments of sorrow, God sees you and is always with you. That was in May 2008.

Then in…

- January 2009, just a few months later, my husband's mom became ill and passed away suddenly. She was in CCU, and family honored her wishes to never be on a vent. She was only in her 60s and still had so much life to live. Our hearts were broken again.
- July 2009, just a few months after that, my husband's father collapsed and passed away suddenly. My husband had been estranged from his dad for years. It seemed they had just been able to establish a true father/son relationship. Then he was gone.
- January 2012, a few years after my dad's passing, my mom became ill and passed away after having had surgery, followed by months of illness and being on hospice. She never really got over dad's passing and battled depression for several years. She asked me once, "Why is God taking so long?" She was ready to go. She told us girls to let her go. My sister and I were there the night she passed.
- In November 2013, a first cousin passed away suddenly.
- In February 2014, another first cousin passed away suddenly. As I sang "I Could Only Imagine" at his funeral, I was numb and could not believe all this had happened.

But for God's grace, our family made it through. No matter how hard it gets, **Hold On!**

Then, as much as you can, and as soon as you can, let the grief give way to memories of their love. If you must, seek support groups and resources that will help you through the loss. Think of what your loved one would want for you. Let that then propel you in moving forward to live in the present. To embrace each new day and to not stay stuck in the sorrow of your loss. We grieve, but not as those who have no hope.

"The Lord is close to the brokenhearted and saves those who are crushed in spirit." **Psalm 34:18 NIV**

For a while, I would see older men and think, why can't my dad still be here? Also, I will never forget the day after my mom passed, when I saw a woman who looked just like her in a grocery store. She had light brown skin and shoulder-length dark hair. I found myself staring at her and wanting to go up and hug her.

Moments like those I have learned to turn into worship. God, I do not understand, but I choose to trust You. My heart awaits our heavenly reunion.

Chapter 5 – Behind the Door - Loss

Nothing prepares our hearts for the loss of a loved one. Yet, God is an ever-present help in our time of trouble. Through it all, you can trust Him.

Is there a loss in your life that is preventing you from moving forward?

Write a letter of reflection to God – Behind the Door - Loss

Consider it pure joy, my brothers and sisters,

whenever you face trials of many kinds

because you know that the testing of

your faith produces perseverance.

James 1:2-3 NIV

CHAPTER 6: A DOOR OF TEST

This passage seems like a contradiction, does it not? I have already been through enough. Now I am to have joy when I am going through trials, temptations, or tests? It is not always easy to see it that way. Yet, I have come to know that the Lord will not leave me. Nor will He leave you. His gentle reminders let me know that I may be walking through it, but I do not have to camp out there. I am coming out on the other side.

By this time, we had left the Baptist church and were active in a powerful word-of-faith ministry. Things were going well. In fact, we served there for seventeen years. I met and married my spouse there, and we had our girls there. I was on fire in worship and was so honored to lead the congregation in praise and worship.

It took me back, though, when I began to hear the words "come out." My first inclination was to rebuke the devil. This is where we were led and where we would stay. Yet, as I purposed to lean in and listen, I came to understand those instructions were not from the enemy but were in fact from the Lord Himself. I thought we would be there forever and always. The error was obviously in my thinking. This would be one of several divine disruptions in my life from the Lord.

Disruption is defined as a disturbance, to interrupt, or a radical change. Even when it is hard, we must be willing to let Him lead. Even when it seemingly breaks protocol or does not make sense. Sometimes, we cannot hear Him any other way.

At this church, while our services once flowed freely in the spirit and the gifts and manifestations of the Holy Spirit were in abundance, things began to change.

Now, we were required to incorporate singing a hymn every Sunday. Our worship time was set on a schedule, and we could not go over the allotted timeframe. We were also required to only sing an exact number of songs. To cap that off, our songs were limited to only the ones selected by the leadership. We had to ask permission to introduce new songs that were not on the list of pre-approved songs. How could our freedom in God be deduced to this? Something had happened, but it would not come to light until we had long left the ministry.

The more I tried to obey, the more miserable I became. I wanted and needed to be free in worship, and back then, I was radical in my expression. The more radical I became the more leadership would pull in the reigns.

Some specifics are being omitted for the sake of respecting and honoring those that I served. I loved my Pastors, but eventually, it was apparent that the Lord was leading me and my family in a different direction. A final conversation with the Pastor resulted in me asking if he was being led in a more conservative direction. I remember being so nervous asking him about that, but I had to know. He had to be told that if that was the direction, then I was not the worship leader for him. In turn, he told me that I had been taught obedience and to just obey. That response was not enough for me.

I gave three months' notice and, before leaving, helped transition in a new worship director. Personally, I also took a ninety-day sabbatical. This was one of the hardest things I have ever done. To let go of what I loved and was called to do in worship and waiting on the Lord for direction when things were not clear.

On top of that, walking away from those you love and care about is so very hard. We were family. However, many of our relationships would discontinue because it was perceived that we were leaving the faith, and to some degree, we were shunned.

This lesson, however, prepared me for the next time God instructed us to move and for the next time God would again require me to lay down what I loved.

He was letting me know He is God, and I had to take Him out of whatever box of experience I had placed Him in. I now understand that God is forward-thinking. He is active, alive, progressive, and moving. He never wants us to stay stuck in a place, a tradition, or to cower from anything or anyone.

"For I know the plans I have for you declares the Lord, plans to prosper you and not to harm you, plans to give you a hope and a future." **Jeremiah 29:11 NIV**

He has "plans" for us, more than one. What I learned is that God's plans are always best, no matter the sacrifice.

If He is dealing with you about coming out of a toxic relationship, or changing your circle of friends that have you stuck in a cycle of sin, or maybe changing your job, or possibly even moving to another state (the latter is coming); whatever it is, He is a sovereign God. Allow Him to have control.

Anything I ever thought I gave up was so much better than I could have ever imagined on the other side of obedience. On the other side of it, I found my reward. Thank you, Lord, for your dealings with my heart. Thank you for your patience until we give you a real "yes!"

Is the heavenly Father speaking to you about anything? Lord, please do not let us be afraid of the cost or back away from the risk of change. Someone said it like this: Partial obedience is still disobedience.

We eventually left that church disappointed and disillusioned, yet God had so much more in store for us.

Our "yes" must be to go all the way with Him.

Chapter 6 – Behind the Door – Tests

Tests and trials are inevitable. We all face them. Personally, I have never liked taking tests, so I only want to have to take it one time.

What has the Lord spoken to you that you have not acted upon? No one else knows, but you do.

Write a letter of reflection to God – Behind the Door - Tests

Jesus Christ is the same yesterday

and today and forevermore.

Hebrews 13:8 NIV

CHAPTER 7: A DOOR OF CHANGE

To some degree, we are all creatures of comfort and sometimes avoid change. However, loss, loneliness, tests and trials let me see my life through a different lens. What was really the priority? I now know that it is to love, to be loved, and to make the most of the time we have with family and friends while here on the earth. We only pass this way once. I now know and understand the importance of positioning myself in a place of total obedience to the Lord so I can be impactful in the lives of others.

Seriously, there have been so many doors…

- Honoring our covenant in marriage. Learning how to disagree agreeably.
- Hurdling the many years my spouse was an Executive Chef and worked 60+ hours per week as I cared for our girls alone.

- Raising our girls and surviving homework, school projects, monthly book reports, parent meetings, and volunteering hours at different school events. Sometimes, it felt like I was in school.
- Raising our girls and disagreeing on how to discipline them. He would insist they stay up at night and finish their school assignments, no matter how late it was or if they were crying uncontrollably because they were tired. I would want them to eat, take baths, go to bed, and wake up early the next morning to finish, if necessary.
- Maneuvering through the ever-changing sea of learning them individually and what they were bent toward.
- Sibling rivalry that could be intense at times. Our house would be so loud with everyone vying to be heard.
- Surviving sports and summers when both our girls played competitive softball but on different teams. He would take one to her practice and game, and I would take the other. It would entail very long days by the time you add the travel time there. Some of their softball games would be as far as an hour away.
- Surviving the years when they became resistant to our instruction. They thought we were old and did not understand.

- Surviving college with our girls (this is a chapter by itself). Who were their friends? Where were they? Sometimes, receiving panicked phone calls due to car issues or "the assignment is due soon, and I need help." We insisted our girls choose colleges no further than three hours away in case the need came up for us to go there. It happened more than once. Also, the countless move-in and move-out times at the end of a semester.
- Hurdling our own job losses and the stress of financial hardships.
- Surviving the time of a family tragedy where a hit-and-run auto accident left my nephew paralyzed from the waist down, and he almost died. I will never forget the telephone call and the rush to the hospital. The first words out of my mouth were that, "He would not die, but live to declare what the Lord had done." Vigils at his bedside and sitting in the CCU waiting room with other families who faced their own crisis. Praise God. He did survive!
- Letting God change our course when we thought we had everything on lock of how it should be.

The one constant in all of this was the word of God and the Lord's faithfulness. During some of this time, we were privileged to partner with and serve in another amazing church for nineteen years. We were led there by the spirit of the Lord after departing from the previous ministry.

We found this church one day in the Yellow Pages while we were at home. Side note: It is no longer the Yellow Pages; today, it is Google. Our plan was to visit every church in the city if necessary. What we did not know is that on the very first day we visited, God would deeply speak to our hearts.

He said to me, "You do not have time to be wounded," or what some would call church hurt from the previous ministry. There was Kingdom work to do, and we had to press forward in Him.

I truly love the local church, and getting reconnected meant everything to me. It had been 90 days since I led worship, and leading worship at this new place was at a whole different level. The freedom to express worship the way it was in my heart felt so good. Then, that was coupled with the joy of starting a children's choir, and we also began to serve in prison outreach ministry together.

I am so very grateful for the leadership of that ministry and the many years of service there. When we left after nineteen years, our Pastor tearfully laid his hands of blessing on me and prayed. My Pastor's wife knelt and blessed my feet. I fought back tears. It was so bittersweet.

By this time, my spouse had already left for Tennessee, our next destination. My heart was torn, and to be honest, it did not quite make sense in the natural to make this move. But God!

This change entailed moving from our home state (we were born and raised there) to another state that we had only traveled through in the past.

It required letting go of everything. Instead of ninety minutes away, we would now be eight hours away from our girls. We resigned from our jobs, sold our home in one weekend, and said goodbye to family and an amazing inner circle of friends. There was such a mix of emotions, but it felt right to follow my spouse's lead in his job and face our new adventure together.

Before leaving, I had heard the Lord say, "There's more." Those words came during a high service, and He moved tremendously. But isn't that just like God? To interrupt what we feel we are in control of.

I needed the change. I had grown comfortable and stagnant with the box I had placed God in. I wanted a renewed passion in my pursuit of Him. It was not that I did not love the Lord, nor that I was not serving. Yet, something was missing, and I knew it. When you are in that place, you can either settle there or press for more.

What I learned is that God was not looking for my comfort but for my conformity. Would I obey? Will you obey?

I thought back to a prayer in which I had asked God for a change. What I was not prepared for was that He would answer that prayer with yet another disruption…one that would shake me to my core.

Chapter 7 – Behind the Door - Change

Disruption is defined as a disturbance or problems that interrupt an event, activity, or process; radical change; to wreck, to ruin.

Can disruption be a good thing? Explain why.

Write a letter of reflection to God – Behind the Door - Change

But those who wait on the Lord shall renew their strength. They shall mount up with wings like eagles, they shall run and not be weary, they shall walk and not faint.

Isaiah 40:31 NKJV

CHAPTER 8: A DOOR OF SOLITUDE

This door has been like no other. When we left our home to move to another state, if you had told me several months later that there would still not be a deep sense of connection, I would not have believed you. I could see glimpses of what He was orchestrating, but not everything. Let me pause here and say, for what I did see, my heart does say, thank you, Lord.

How I missed my "inner circle" and that sense of community. This loss due to relocation really hit me hard. Yes, there were telephone calls, texts, cards, letters, and Zoom was an option, but it was not the same.

In fact, to some degree, we had all been isolated for months due to the pandemic with Covid and now this move. The depth of my feeling alone became greater than I can articulate—day after day of being home alone. My spouse would leave for work, and I was in a city where I knew no one. I even recall a time when I said out loud, "Why does it have to be so hard?"

I wrote letters to potential employers and applied for jobs with no response, or I would receive responses of, "We've chosen another candidate." At that time, I did not share with my spouse how serious it was because he was handling the pressure of a new job.

So, how do I get to where I am okay with being alone and with my own thoughts? There must be a purpose in this season. I began to pray and talk to the Lord about it.

Solitude can be defined as simply being alone. And yet, we have this promise:

"I will not in any way fail you, nor give you up, nor leave you without support." **Hebrews 13:5 AMPC**

I went back to what I knew but somehow had slipped away from, and that is very simply sitting in His presence, no agenda, just being with Him and trusting He was with me. You may ask, how long did you sit? Well, it varied. At first, a few minutes seemed like forever. I tried not to be distracted by time. I would stay until I was no longer distracted in my mind by anything else. I would stay until I felt His presence.

For some, I know being alone can be frightening. However, I began to find a sense of comfort and to be at peace again. You can, too. I was no longer worrying about the outcome or consumed with busyness. Let tomorrow handle itself. My one desire came to be to want to be with the Lord.

Now that I am on the other side of this struggle let me submit to you that it does get better. If you find yourself there, know that He will be faithful.

At the end of myself, I remembered when the Lord spoke to my heart and said, "Go back to piano." This was years prior. I had taken piano lessons for a time, got bored, and quit. As an adult student, I simply did not want to learn songs that I did not like. Plus, the method of reading music seemed entirely too tedious.

At church, we always had amazing musicians who played by ear. I wanted to be able to accompany myself in my private time of worship. I would tinker with it from time to time but lacked the discipline to stick with it.

I would ask other musicians for shortcuts in learning. Is anybody else looking for a shortcut in life? Shortcuts will seemingly present an opportunity to go around, but that is not always the best choice.

Eventually, I found an online method to play worship piano by chords. How amazing it was to find that most songs comprised of only a few chords, and there was a repetitive pattern to how they were played. I searched for and found individuals I could understand their teaching method and then purchased an online piano series. The chord method was a game-changer for me. Once I started again, my ability to learn and grow in playing was much better. What did I have to lose? I had nothing but time now, right?

My perspective of being alone changed. I could either resist it or embrace it. Being alone and loneliness took on new meaning. I was not alone because the Lord was with me. He was teaching me mastery over it when loneliness would come.

Now, I have learned to welcome and embrace my alone time. It is like a guest that you have who comes unannounced. While it may have been unplanned, the joy of their fellowship and time together makes you want to invite them back again.

In my place of solitude, I would simply worship and pray. I would also journal, read, or sit in silence and listen for His voice. Sometimes, I merely waited in His presence. I now have a precious little spot in my home that is deemed my place with the Lord. When I go there, it is priceless.

So, this was the purpose. To find Him all over again. Now, I am starting to understand.

I did not realize how I had allowed my life to be driven by so many other factors, such as busyness, work, and pleasing others. The constant bombardment of needing to do something was relentless back home. Did I even know how to be still before?

He has now become my audience of One. It does not matter if my voice cracks as I sing or if I make a mistake on the piano. In this place of solitude, I have learned how to find His presence again. My joy has been renewed. My strength has been revitalized. Thank you, Jesus.

My soul desperately needed this season of rest, and I did not even realize it. I was working for several years at a Level 1, 500-bed trauma hospital with endless traumas, codes, deaths, emotional distress, and topped with working through the pandemic. It had taken its toll. My soul needed redirecting to my first love. In my waiting is where I found Him again.

After many months, I knew I had found my renewal when I stood in the kitchen. I was not praying or asking God for anything when suddenly, His presence enveloped me, and tears began to fall. I felt such a sense of peace and gratitude.

I would go through it all again to have this sweet spot that I have found in the Lord, for the stripping away of everything that exposed my neediness and drew me to Him.

"Hear my cry, O God; listen to my prayer. From the ends of the earth, I call to you, I call as my heart grows faint; lead me to the rock that is higher than I." **Psalm 61:1-2 NIV**

Thank you, Lord, for hearing my cry.

Some beautiful yet simple choruses that I learned to play and worship to in His presence are:

"As the Deer" by M. Nystrom

"Waiting on You" by C. Brown

"Withholding Nothing" by W. McDowell

"More than Anything" by L. Campbell

"Joy of My Desire" by Hosanna Music

"Nothing Else" by C. Carnes

This is to name a few. No, I will not be the next great pianist, nor do I aspire to be. But, oh my, the moments of having a sense of His nearness have been priceless.

The glorious moments as I sit to sing and play (sometimes bursting out in applause, in laughter, or in tears) for my audience of One have forever marked me. Because honestly, nothing else matters.

The world presents so many distractions. We can spend hours scrolling through various social media platforms, being entertained by the seemingly perfect lives of others as we look at their filtered pictures.

Yet, somehow, we have so little time for the one thing we were created for…to know Him and to be known by Him. Time is the one thing we can never get back once it has passed. I am learning to embrace the moments with Him. I am so grateful my days are now filled with longing to be with Him. I am hungry again.

I pray that when reading these words, something also stirs in you.

"As the deer pants for streams of water, so my soul pants for you, O God. My soul thirsts for God, for the living God. When can I go and meet with God?" **Psalm 42:1-2 NIV**

I still have my "inner circle" of friends, and I can see a glimpse of friendships here in Tennessee, too, but in the meantime, my heart chooses not to be anxious.

I used to always say, what is next? Now, I am not as quick to skip past things. My heart is to live in the moment and let the Lord surprise me with His plan.

I want to challenge you. If your life does not feel satisfying or feels chaotic and full of drama, it is time for a change. You may have even said it before, "I never have time." However, you do have the time and the power within yourself to make that change.

Let me suggest that you reevaluate your priorities. What consumes your time? Is it TV, recreation, social media? Give place to what really matters. I began to monitor how much TV I was watching. I did not say that I do not watch TV. In fact, I am a sports enthusiast, and I watch the NBA and MLB, especially during playoffs. Yay, team, go! So, it is not that you cannot watch TV; it is how much you are watching. Time that can never again be captured once it has passed.

Consider something more positive, like a walk, listening to an inspiring podcast, reading a book, or journaling. I have discovered my love for reading again. However, that did not happen until I prioritized some things. Possibly, there is an author in you. I can imagine that the Lord has been nudging you about something. Would you agree that it is time to get started?

I promise you the reward is peace and joy in His presence. The reward is less anxiety and stress over endless world events and catastrophes. The reward is a sense of confidence as you approach your day knowing He is in control. Put Him first!

"You will keep in perfect peace all who trust in you, all whose thoughts are fixed on you." **Isaiah 26:3 NLT**

We need peace now more than ever. I find that as I look to Him, I am more readily apt to pray for others or be sensitive to their needs. Take another look. We are surrounded by hurting people—people battling sickness, loss, depression, and mental health crises. We can be the answer to that need if we ourselves are not distracted.

You do not have to be a minister or have a title to be there for someone else. All you must be is a willing vessel.

You have the time. Please understand that waiting is not being idle, but it is actively participating with God in what you are expecting. Guard against distractions. He can be found when we seek Him with all our heart.

Chapter 8 – Behind the Door – Solitude

I am amazed that the Creator of the universe gives audience to me and that I can come before His presence and wait there to hear His heart.

What are some things that are a distraction for you?

Write a letter of reflection to God – Behind the Door - Solitude

Those of us who are strong and able in faith need to step in and lend a hand to those who falter, and not just do what is most convenient for us. Strength is for service, not status. Each one of us needs to look after the good of the people around us, asking ourselves, "How can I help?"

Romans 15:1 MSG

CHAPTER 9: A DOOR OF CHAPLAINCY

It is early Saturday morning. My spouse has gone fishing for striped bass, and I am sitting on our screened-in deck. The birds are chirping, there is a slight breeze, and the sun is shining. I honestly felt like I could have slept a little longer, but more than that, I have come to yearn for these quiet moments with God. Typically for me, I have a cup of caramel vanilla coffee, my devotional, and my journal.

Things have changed so drastically over the last few months. In fact, if you would have asked me this time last year where we would be, it certainly would not have been to be here. We now reside in a new state, at a new church, and I am at a new hospital in my 8th year of chaplaincy.

As my mind began to reflect on the many patient encounters I have experienced over the years, I was flooded with thoughts of what was "Behind the Door" in those situations. I began to write.

My chaplaincy journey started several years ago. I had begun to have feelings of unrest while doing what I loved most: leading worship at church. I heard the words "there's more" right in the middle of a worship service. I should have been satisfied. What "more" could I want? Yet, I hid those words in my heart. I knew that God would bring clarity to what He was saying.

As I began to pray and seek the Lord about it, so many things came together: the right introductions to key people and now knowledge of a Clinical Pastoral Education (CPE) program. I applied and awaited a response. I was so overjoyed at being accepted. My official classroom training and clinical hours began in August 2015.

Those two words of "there's more" would take me on an adventure in the Lord I never dreamed possible.

Innate in me has always been a heart for hurting people, but I knew nothing about the clinical side of that. My first mentor was amazing. She was not afraid to allow me to step into the role of being lead page. A page to the ED for an emergency, a page to a patient room for a Code, another page because someone was requesting a Bible or prayer, meeting people as you walk through the hospital who appeared lost and giving them directions.

Oh, and did I mention these were happening all at once? My mentor at the hospital taught me how to triage, and it helped propel me to learn quickly. She affirmed that I would find my own rhythm and that there was already grace and hospitality in me to connect with people. I am forever grateful to her for that.

A Chaplain can simply be defined as one who provides spiritual guidance and pastoral care to patients and their families in need. What an honor it has been.

***"How beautiful on the mountains are the feet of those who bring good news, who proclaim peace, who bring good tidings, who proclaim salvation, who say to Zion, "Your God reigns!"* Isaiah 52:7 NIV**

This door would be one that God would use for me to comfort others like I had received comfort when my dad was ill many years before.

I have a dear friend who has often stated, "I do not know how you do it." My girls have even said, "I do not know how you can be in so many tragic situations every day. But, if I need a Chaplain, you are the one for me."

Very simply, it fits me. It is God's calling and a passion only He can give. It is His grace alone for every patient and family.

Behind the Door started with thoughts of my many patient encounters. It is the reason for these writings.

In general, and with specifics purposely omitted, I wanted to list a few of the patient encounters I have had over the years. As these thoughts flooded my mind, there were so many that I could not write fast enough. As you read them, envision with me God's heart of compassion toward each one:

- Patients sitting up happy and saying, "Come on in," because they anticipate discharge that day.
- Patients with family gathered at the bedside, tearful and facing a decision of hospice that day for their loved one.
- Patients with spouse on the telephone. Fear and concern that the patient would not be able to be cared for at home upon release. They do not know what to do. Prayer with them over the telephone.
- Patients who have passed and a grieving spouse. Facing the agony of telling the kids.
- Patients with a critical diagnosis and all they want is to tell their story and be heard. Sitting with them, providing presence, and listening.
- Patients who are confused and estranged from family. Asking, "Is God with me? Does he love me?"

- Patients in hospice, lying in bed, and non-responsive. Their eyes opening briefly as I speak words of comfort and blessing over them. Eternity awaits.
- Patients with a serious diagnosis but wanting to fight and not give up. The family weary and in disagreement.
- Patients of fetal demise and no family present. In tears and inconsolable.
- Patients married 30, 40, and even 50 years, and the spouse at the bedside of their loved one, uncertain of what to do or how they will face the future alone.
- Patients of no faith not wanting my presence or prayer. Yet, the importance of really seeing them and being there even if only briefly.
- Patients in CCU and family visiting or camped out for days. Some want to wait, and other family wants to let their loved one go.
- Patients anxious about an upcoming procedure.
- Patients who are elderly, tearful, and have no family support.
- Patients who are young, yet despite their age, they are in critical condition.
- Patients being released but grieving the recent loss of a spouse and no one to go home to.

- Patients in isolation due to Covid and praying with the family over the telephone on the other side of a glass door.
- Patients that I visited days before now on comfort care. A well-timed follow-up visit and within minutes of praying, the patient passes.
- Patients who face their diagnosis with faith and courage, yet they know they will not be here by the next holiday.
- Patients who pass, triggering the family as they remember others who have gone before.
- Patients who are grateful and pray for me, thanking me for what I do and that I cared and had stopped by.

These examples are simply a few over the years. There are so many more. I have cried with them and been their shoulder to cry on. My heart cherishes each one.

A Chaplain has the privilege to show presence, listen, provide emotional and family support and affirmation, give hope, administer sacraments, offer comfort, share scriptures, and provide prayer.

"And that you may love the Lord your God, listen to his voice, and hold fast to him. For the Lord is your life..."
Deuteronomy 30:20 NIV

My desire is, Lord as your vessel, help me to silence all the other noise so your words and thoughts of life arise in me for every patient. How I need You so that I can see beyond my own limitations and continue to care for the needs of others. I want to feel what they feel. I want to see what they see.

My heart says yes, in Jesus' name. Amen!

Chapter 9 – Behind the Door – Chaplaincy

Have you come to a place of resolve over what the Lord is asking of you?

What is your "yes" before the Lord?

Write a letter of reflection to God – Behind the Door - Chaplaincy

I am convinced and confident of this very thing, that He who has begun a good work in you will continue to perfect and complete it until the day of Christ Jesus, the time of His return.

Philippians 1:6 AMP

CHAPTER 10: A DOOR OF "DO IT AGAIN" LORD

My journey to "Do It Again" is full of amazing blessings and surprises from the heart of God. The blessings far outweigh the hardships and times when I felt it was over. Precious moments in Him that have left me speechless because He had answered prayers beyond my expectations. Moments where I was on the floor weeping from an overwhelming sense of His presence as His love surrounded me. Moments when He would whisper to my heart, "You are my girl," and that is all I needed to hear to keep going. Times when He would allow me to be a vessel to turn someone else who was lost toward the hope that can only be found in Him. Isn't that just like God?

The nine-hour drive from my former state to where we reside now, gave me time to reflect and remember. I noticed the terrain began to change and it went from mainly cornfields and straight highways, to winding roads, drop offs, hills, mountains and valleys. It spoke to me of the changes that had already begun. Everything would be different. I found myself whispering a prayer, God will you "Do It Again?" Will you show up again?

The revelation is that I do not have to look for what is next. I am living it. The Lord has proven Himself time and time again. When I knew no one in Tennessee and found myself wanting to give up, His love would compel me to keep going. He has opened so many doors.

Initially, the struggle was real. Not knowing anyone and essentially starting over was hard. The emptiness I felt making me question "Am I losing my mind?" I had never felt this way before and that question shocked me. And yet when I felt I had hit a wall these words that follow came. While looking out the back door of our house, I saw cows lying in the field and a mountain in the backdrop, commanding attention. A prophetic word that has come to pass in this present season in a very rich way:

"I am the God who can command one thing to lay down and another to stand up. Whatever you need I can sort that out. You do not need to figure it out or fix anything. Even in some areas as you face what feels like uncertainty, I am yet God. I got this! Focus and lean in, as in this season I am

speaking and pouring out my Spirit. Doors, surprises, more doors, and more surprises are what I have in store for those who love Me and walk upright. I have been with you even when you felt lonely, even when you questioned what if or why. I am even here with you now in this moment. You are my girl. People, places, and things are being aligned. I will be faithful to perform what I promised. Be assured it is done!"

Those words comforted me when I still did not know things would work out. Have you ever been there? Are you even possibly there now? He is a God who specializes in the impossible. I believe He will make a way for you just like He did for me.

Eventually, a new job, church family, friendships and community would all begin to unfold. The revelation for me is that right here is my "Do It Again" season. It's not somewhere far off. My blessed place is right now and is being manifested even as I type these words.

So, at this point, I have concluded that I give up! No, it is not what you think. I am not giving up my belief and trust in the Lord. Life is way too precious for that. Yet, I choose not to squander the high price that was paid for me to have victory. I will not miss it this time with unbelief.

In these "seasoned" years of my life (my best years) what I choose to do is to give up having to figure everything out. I give up having to be in control. I do not have to have an agenda for tomorrow or boxes to check off. All I need is the One who holds my tomorrow.

I ask myself sometimes, and maybe you have too, have I ever been disappointed? The answer is yes. In fact, I have disappointed myself more than once. However, the disappointment is not because God has not been faithful. Even in my disappointment, God has been so kind and patient with me. He waited until I came to my senses, repented, and turned around—even when I planned to sin. Does anybody want to admit that? Even when I broke my promise, He did not break His. Thank you, Lord for your forgiveness and mercy.

So, a few things I choose to give up:

- Worry about my life
- Worry about my girls or my spouse
- Worry about tomorrow
- Focus on worldly ambitions
- Fussing
- Complaining
- Resisting

I choose to give Him these seasoned years: the thoughts of getting older that sometimes cross my mind with knees that ache at times, the gray hair that must be colored every six to eight weeks, the wrinkles that I promise you were not there yesterday. Even the sense that I do not move as fast as I used to up and down the stairs. Need I say more? Well, He can have it all. Whatever I have not figured out by now, I will release to His sovereignty and very simply keep pressing. The joy and privilege is found in just having today. In that, I will be grateful. One of my favorite passages:

"Trust in the Lord with all your heart, and lean not on your own understanding; In all your ways acknowledge Him, and He will direct your paths." **Proverbs 3:5-6 NKJV**

I see this season of my life almost like a 4x100 relay race. The lead-off runner is very important because they set the pace and hopefully run well enough to put the team in the lead.

The second and third legs are equally important. The handoffs must be with precision. They must run well so as not to forfeit the lead. They must stay in their lane and not impede anyone else's race. Yet, the key person to watch for, the one we are all excited about and believe will bring it home is the anchor. You cannot drop the baton now. The anchor must have the end goal in mind and run full out. They must have the strength and stamina to take it across the finish line.

I feel like that is me in this season. I am the anchor. As the Lord pushes and paces me, I have found my rhythm in Him. I choose to run full out with complete abandonment for His will alone.

Is this possibly what the Lord is dealing with you about? To finish well!

However long I have left, I will trust Him.

Whichever way He leads, I will follow.

When He calls me, I will answer.

I speak over my life that I have another run in me. Come on, Lord. Do what only you can do. This is no time to look back. Very simply, I am ready. I am yours. I choose to stay focused and to finish well.

As I write these pages, I would never have believed I could come this far. As I write these pages, I now clearly understand that new chapters will bring new challenges. Well, so be it because whatever is, ***Behind the Door***, my reliance is upon the Lord.

Let me ask you, have you opened the door of your heart to receive Christ's love? He loves you so much that He gave His life on the cross for the forgiveness of your sins.

"For God so greatly loved and dearly prized the world, that He even gave His one and only begotten Son, so that whoever believes and trusts in Him as Savior shall not perish, but have eternal life." **John 3:16 AMP**

I present Christ to you. Receiving His gift of salvation will set you on the course of the greatest adventure in life. I did not say it would be an easy life or one without hardships. Yet, a key to this adventure is in knowing that no matter what you face, He is always with you.

Please pause for a moment, believe, and say this prayer with me if you do not know Him in the free pardon of your sin:

"Jesus, I believe in you. I need you and I ask you to forgive me of my sin. Come into my heart and live in me. Help me to live for you. Thank you for forgiving me. Right now, I am safe. Right now, I am saved. In Jesus, name. Amen!"

If you prayed that prayer, congratulations! Your race has just begun.

Chapter 10 – Behind the Door – "Do it Again" Lord

Can you clearly see right now what He is doing in your life? Embrace your now and He will take care of your next. The Lord has victory in mind for you. Consider that right now is your "Do it Again" season.

What is it that you would like for God to do in your life in this season?

Write a letter of reflection to God – Behind the Door – "Do It Again"

CONCLUSION

"Ask and keep on asking and it will be given to you; seek and keep on seeking and you will find; knock and keep on knocking and the door will be opened to you." **Matthew 7:7-11 AMP**

In conclusion, I believe we can never be finished asking, seeking, or knocking. What we need most is more of His presence and power in our lives. The key is not to fear what is on the other side of the door. God is with us. He is for us. This journey, adventure, and life in Him is one I would absolutely do all over again.

I confess that the only time I have ever gotten tripped up is when I took my focus off the Lord and looked to someone or something else.

One of my favorite songs is "Keeper of the Door" by artists David and Nicole Binion. I have found my place in Him, and there is no other place I would rather be.

"For a day in Your courts is better than a thousand anywhere else; I would rather stand as a doorkeeper at the threshold of the house of my God than to live at ease in the tents of wickedness." **Psalm 84:10 AMP**

It is my prayer for you that whatever door you face, you will have the courage to go through it and the grace to cling to His promises. The door is there for you to get to the next place, the next season, the next level. Or possibly the door is there for you to wait. He will show you.

If you find yourself in a difficult place right now, you are in good company. Even Christ endured. I promise you it will not last forever. While the enemy will tell you what you face is impossible, what he does not say is that you can come out! On the other side of what you face is the door that leads to better. It leads to greater. I believe that for you.

***"Now to him who is able to do immeasurably more than all we ask or imagine, according to his power that is at work within us."* Ephesians 3:20 NIV**

Surrender. He is calling you. The door of surrender is the only one that leaves you with no regrets. He is the prize for your heart's open door.

I am excited to say that I have begun to get a glimpse of our next adventure as we enter…

"In The Room" … God bless you!

ABOUT THE AUTHOR

Dee Pulliam has served in the local church for over thirty-five years and has been an ordained minister since 1990. She is a wife, mother, minister, worship leader, and chaplain.

Dee has completed eight-hundred hours of Clinical Pastoral Education (CPE) training through the Association for Clinical Pastoral Education (ACPE). Most of her chaplaincy years have been served at a Level 1, 500-bed Trauma Center. Dee is now serving in her eighth year as a hospital chaplain.

Dee has served in leadership roles as minister of music, on various committees, facilitated women's groups, and taught and preached the word.

For over twenty-five years, Dee has volunteered in ministry at various state and county correctional facilities for incarcerated men and women.

The passion of her heart is always to bring light in the darkness. The anointing is evident as she teaches the uncompromised word of God with clarity and boldness and the richness of His presence as she leads in worship.

Since 1985, Dee has been married to her husband, Raven Pulliam, and resides in Knoxville, TN. They have two beautiful daughters, Raven Breanna and Tiara Christine.

OTHER REV/12 PUBLICATIONS

In ***There's No Place Like Home: Discovering the Destiny Within***, pastor and teacher Daryl W. Arnold unpacks biblical truths that will encourage and empower you to pursue your God-given destiny. Using the classic story, The Wizard of Oz and its unique characters, Pastor Arnold paints a picture of the journey we all take as we discover God's purpose for our lives, the challenges we experience on the way and just how deeply this journey changes us. This combination book and study guide, designed for individual or group reflection, will not only encourage and entertain you, it will provide practical steps toward pursuing the abundant life God has for you, a life that far exceeds anything you could ask for or imagine.

If you are going to be a mature Christian that produces Godly results, you must be rooted and connected with the person of the Holy Spirit. In this book and study guide, pastor and teacher Daryl W. Arnold offers practical disciplines and strategies on how to develop a real and genuine relationship with the power, presence and yes, the personality of God's Spirit. In ***Holy Spirit Ignored No More – A Formal Introduction to the God in You***. You are formally introduced to the God in you. After reading this book and going through this study guide, it is the prayer of the author that what you have known in the past as the Fire of God, you will come to know as a Friend from God.

Not Yet Released is a condensed story highlighting the testimonies of a young lady seeking to succeed in life. Her frustrations, strongholds, and struggles begin to all make sense as God takes her on a journey that will change her life forever. God has used the writing of this book as a tool to bring her into promise. As you read this book you will discover: Who God is to you, God's design for relationships, How God has been operating behind the scenes, The Key to Good Success, The Power of the Cross, The Importance of Deliverance to your Future, and Jesus in your story. This book is a God's story just for you!

In Ephesians 6, Paul is writing a letter to the Church of Ephesus encouraging them to stand firm as they go through some of the toughest times in their Christian journey. He is first acknowledging that God has confirmed their salvation, empowered them to be victorious, and called them to greatness. Yet they will still have to overcome the schemes of the devil in the process. The Apostle Paul uses the image of a Roman soldier's armor as a tangible example of how we can arm ourselves against the evil one. Through this Inductive Teaching Series study guide, pastor and teacher Daryl W. Arnold's prayer is that the study of these scriptures will prepare you for spiritual warfare, propel you into your God given purpose and prevent you from giving up during the process.

Christians throughout the world often use the blood of Jesus to overcome their adversity but neglect to use their testimony as a bridge to their breakthrough. ***The Word of Our Testimony - Treasures from Broken Vessels***, is a series of short topical devotions that are written with the purpose of bringing encouragement to the discouraged, hope to the hopeless, help to the helpless and to once again set the fire of faith to those who feel spiritually burned out. Allow these candid testimonies from broken men, women, and children of diverse backgrounds to stir up the gifts of God that have been lying dormant within.

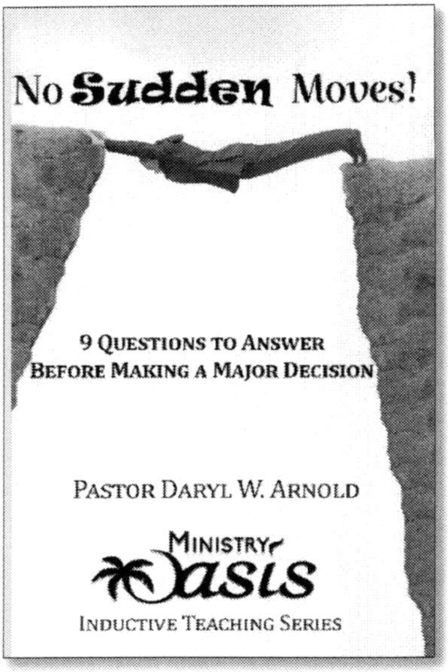

Life is a series of decisions that need to be made in order to fulfill the purpose God has prepared for us. The problem is that sometimes knowing what decision to make can be hard to discern and sometimes even harder to do. Prayerfully, this Inductive Teaching Series will equip you to lean on these nine steps of wisdom to assist you in moving in the right direction. No matter how anxious you may be to make that decision, resist the temptation to move forward until you have answered all nine of these critical questions.

There is a battle in the heavenlies over the faith of men. Jesus declares in Luke 18:6-8 when the Son of Man comes will He find faith on the earth? Isaiah cries out, "Whose report will you believe (Isaiah 53:1)?" Will you believe the report of the Lord or the report of the world? Elijah asked the children of Israel on the Mount of Carmel, "How long will you halt between two opinions? If the Lord be God, follow Him, but if Baal, then follow him (1 Kings 18:21)." We need to make up our minds who we will believe. I believe that this is the crux of the cosmic battle that is going on, the battle for the faith of the hearts of men, women, boys, and girls. In this book, you will learn principles that will teach you how to stop being defeated and just surviving in life, to overcoming and winning in life.

Yes!! God still speaks! ***Quips, Quotes, and Conversations with God*** are a compilation of conversations between the author, Evangelist Sonji Patterson, and God. Moments that she had encountered as she went along her day, week, or month. Moments that have developed her on her spiritual walk.

Remember, God made a promise. He said that He would never forsake you. God is the real "Ride or Die" (Psalm 55:22), and He is no respecter of persons (Acts 10:34). There are many moments in Quips, Quotes, and Conversations with God that you will be able to grab onto for your own personal use, so with highlighter and pencil on hand: Enjoy!

***"Children are a heritage from the Lord, offspring a reward from him. Like arrows in the hands of a warrior are children born in one's youth."* Psalms 127:3-4 NIV**

This book is written by the inheritance of the Lord, the next generation. As you turn each page of this devotion, you will discover that the anointing of God does not just rest upon the seasoned saints, but it also rests upon the hearts of simple, yet intelligent children. You will hear the raw, real and resurrecting testimonies of young lions that have been called and compelled to usher in the next, end time revival. Brace yourselves as you experience the manifested presence of God through this living document of literature legacy, ***The Word of Our Testimony, The Text Generation***.

~Pastor Daryl W. Arnold

Healing the Brokenhearted with a God of Understanding was birthed through my pain, shame, past failures, and hang-ups. The purpose of this book is to bring healing to a nation. We must learn that we are purposed for God's journey here on earth and not our own. Everything that we have gone through; the good the bad and the ugly, was all necessary for growth and maturity but most of all for His Glory. Whatever your place of brokenness is, never allow it, nor people, to define you. Don't allow jackets that you don't fit to be put on you or put you in a place that you cannot blossom, grow, or heal. God will never bring you to a thing and not bring you through a thing. Jeremiah 29:11 NIV says, "For I know the plans I have for you declares the Lord, plans to prosper you, and not harm you, plans to give you hope and a future."

Made in USA
Knoxville, TN
23 August 2024